THE EMPLOYEE ENTREPRENEUR

HOW TO START A SUCCESSFUL SIDE BUSINESS AND MAKE EXTRA MONEY WITHOUT QUITTING YOUR DAY JOB

INCLUDES

33 PROVEN AND EASY TO START
BUSINESS IDEAS YOU CAN START TODAY USING YOUR PROFESSIONAL EXPERIENCE

EMMANUEL AMETSI

DISCLAIMER
The information shared in this book is not intended as a substitute for professional advice. The views expressed are those of the author alone, and should not be taken as expert instruction or commands. The Reader is responsible for his or her own actions

CONTACT THE AUTHOR
Mobile: +233242107400
Email: Emmanuel.ametsi@gmail.com Instagram: emm_ametsi
LinkedIn: Emmanuel Ametsi

Published by BKC Publishing info@BKC.name
Tel: +233244961121

Dedication

To my Wife, my Queen and my No.1 Motivator.
You've been my source of joy and inspiration.
Thanks for the cheers My Love; REJOICE.
We're Winning Together!!!

Introduction

Financial freedom is a dream for everyone, whether they admit it or not. Even for people who claim not to be moved or swayed by money or earthly things, the reality is that money can make life easier and more enjoyable. We all want to attain different levels of financial freedom. Hence, what satisfies one may not be enough for another. But one thing is sure: we all wish for a time when money won't be a problem. For that period when we can chase our dreams unhindered because money or better said the lack of it is no longer a problem. As much as this is admirable, how can we attain financial freedom?

For many people, financial freedom means being able to retire early and live comfortably on their investments. For others, it means being able to work less and spend more time with their families and friends. And for still others, it means being able to pursue their passions without worrying about money.

Whatever your definition of financial freedom may be, it is something that is achievable with hard work, planning, and discipline.

There are many ways to attain financial freedom. The first amongst them being understanding how money works. The list goes on and on. In recent times, one of the ways to attain financial freedom which has been gaining popularity is using multiple streams of income. In fact, now, it is almost unheard of that anyone who wants to make more money ignores the multiple streams of income principle.

> **It is almost unheard of that anyone who wants to make more money ignores the multiple streams of income principle.**

The principle simply states that one should have more than one source of income that adds on to their main source of income. The catch here is that it must not conflict with your day job which is also known as your 9 to 5. You do not want to lose one source of income for another. You need both. There are many benefits to having multiple streams of income. First, it can help to reduce your risk. If one source of income dries up, you will still have others to rely on. Second, it can help you to grow your wealth faster. When you have more money coming in, you can invest it and grow your wealth over time. Third, it can give you more flexibility and freedom. If you have multiple streams of income, you can choose to work less or retire early.

The advent and advancement of technology has made it possible and seamless for one to do more than one job at a time. One can have a thriving business online and still be an employee in an organisation without any of them having to suffer.

This book is a guide that explains the concept of side hustling, some side hustles worth venturing into, the skills you need to excel, the cost involved and the profits one may get from these ventures. Dig in and make some money on the side!

Chapter One

THE CONCEPT OF 9 - 5

Did you know that before the 20th century, an employee was required to work for 10 to 12 hours a day? In fact, in the Industrial revolution, employees worked for 16 hours each day. Soon enough, workers started protesting against the long hours of work. Welsh social reformer, Owen Welsh, led this campaign for the eight-hour work day. In 1926, Henry Ford of Ford Motors Company issued a 5-day, 40-hour workweek for its workers. The Fair Labour Acts Standards Act of 1938 in the USA made it official by limiting working hours to 44 hours in a week. This was later changed to 40 work hours a week in 1940.

That was a brief history of how we came about the 8 working hours a day which equals 40 working hours a week. This is what many of us came to know as work. A 9-5 worker is someone who works a traditional office job, typically from 9am to 5pm, from Monday through to Friday, where the name comes from. A typical 9-5 worker does not go to work on public holidays. Over the years, there have been calls to relook at the concept as many are seeking for flexible hours.

There are several advantages to being a 9-5 worker. First on that list is that, it provides a sense of predictability and stability. The hours are mostly set which works well for an employee as it makes it easier to plan one's life. In most traditional settings, working outside of working hours comes with some monetary reward.

A typical 9-5 comes with certain perks such as health insurance, subsidized lunch packages, paid leave and so much more. Another advantage of working in a traditional office setting is that it provides one with opportunities for networking and professional development.

There are also some downsides to being a 9-5 worker. Just as the hours are stable and predictable, they are also inflexible. Most 9-5 jobs do not bend the time for anyone. A worker is expected to be in at the set time without fail. A worker who has family or other commitments may struggle with balancing them with his or strict working hours.

A 9-5 job can also be pretty boring because it is repetitive. If the work you do does not challenge you, it can be difficult to stay motivated. I believe the worst downside to having a 9-5 is that it can limit you to one source of income. In the current global economic situation, relying on one source of income can be suicidal. Having a single source of income to rely on for all one's financial needs is risky. In the event of any economic upheaval, your source of income can be threatened or lost. Even people who earn six figure salaries are constantly on the look-out for more streams of income.

> **In the current global economic situation, relying on one source of income can be suicidal.**

Chapter Two

THERE'S EXTRA MONEY TO BE MADE

As we already said, money makes life easier and more enjoyable. In the current global economic situation, sticking to one source of income can be suicidal. Having a single source of income to rely on for all one's financial needs is risky. In the event of any economic upheaval, your source of income can be threatened or lost. Even people who earn six figure salaries are constantly on the look-out for more streams of income.

> **People who earn six figure salaries are constantly on the look-out for more streams of income.**

In life, nothing is promised. This minute you are living your best dream; with a good paying job that caters to your every need and want. The next second your entire world comes crumbling and you lose everything you own and hold dear.

In 2020, when the entire globe came to a standstill because of the Covid pandemic, many lost their day jobs. Jobs that they had given their time and resources to. Jobs that they neglected their families for. When the time came for downsizing, they just had to go. The organisations had to choose between that worker and staying in business. Even for companies that did not downsize, business came to a screeching halt which meant there was little to no money trickling in.

This is where earning an extra income from a side hustle comes to the rescue. A side hustle is a job or work you do in addition to your primary job that you get paid for. Earning extra income can completely change one's life from helping you to pay off your debts to helping you live more comfortably than living from pay cheque to pay cheque.

Aside the monetary gains in having a side hustle, it is also a very good way to pursue your passion. As we grow and evolve, we discover new passions that may not necessarily qualify to be our main jobs. A side hustle is a great way to make some money doing something you love.

> **A side hustle is a great way to make some money doing something you love.**

A side hustle can be the best avenue to gain experience and skills in a new area. In fact, there are many stories of people who totally changed to careers they started as a side hustle. This is an option that will work wonders for you if you are interested in gaining any experience outside what you do.

One of the best ways to test run a business idea is to start it as a side hustle. This way, you don't commit yourself fully by quitting your day job to try something that you are unsure of. You can start small and scale up when it picks up.

Fun is another reason to consider starting a side hustle. If you don't truly enjoy your 9-5 job, a side hustle that excites you is an option to consider. Especially in situations where your 9-5 pays well and has many benefits. You can make your stable income in your 9-5 and have fun in your side hustle which generates extra income for you.

Remember that all of these advantages or reasons to have a side hustle adds on to the monetary reward that comes with it. A side hustle should be something you are passionate about. To make it work, you need to invest the time and effort it needs. When you are not passionate about it, it's only a matter of time before it fizzles out.

Chapter Three

TYPES OF INCOME

We work to earn an income. Our long hours of work and service is rewarded with what we call an income. According to Investopedia, income is "the money that a person or an entity receives in exchange for their labour or products." Income is mostly generated from working. However, there are different kinds of income based on how we get the money. It is important to note that income comes in the form of money and nothing else.

Now, what are the types of income. There are many types of income. The basic ones are the passive and active income. There are many other incomes classified under these basic ones. For me, I will categorise income into three main types. They are:

- Earned or active income
- Passive income
- Portfolio or investment income

We will delve into what each of them entails. I must

confess that I grouped them into these three types mainly because of how these incomes are generated.

Earned also known as active income is simply money you make from actively performing a service. It is the money you make from exchanging your time, expertise and effort with an entity, organisation or individual. For earned income, it requires being present and actively working. Remember when your brother paid you to wash his clothes for him? That was active income. Your income was determined by the washing of his clothes by you.

Active income is not only limited to others paying you for working for them. It is also money you pay yourself for working for yourself. If you own a business and actively perform the service for that business, you are earning active income.

Earned income comes in various forms. When your employer pays you on an hourly basis, that is a wage and a form of active income. A salary is also a form of active income which can be paid weekly, biweekly or monthly. Under active income, we also have commissions.

Commission is a percentage of money an employee receives based on the cost of an item or service. For some employees, commission come as an additional earning to their main salaries. For others, commission is their main source of active income. Such people only work based on commission. Any money they earn is the commission of a sale that went through.

Receiving a tip is also another form of active income. A tip is a gift mostly monetary that one offers someone for a service rendered or anticipated. Most waiters, hairdressers, hotel workers and taxi drivers get a lot of money from kind customers who give them tips for the service they render. In fact, the U.S. Department of Labour considers an employee who receives more than $30 in tips as a tipped employee.

Passive income on the other hand is money that you make without actively working. You can literally not lift a finger and earn this type of income. This type of income comes from rental properties. Do you have any property that you are not currently using? Renting that out could earn you some passive income. It could be residential or commercial property; it is good enough to rake in some money.

Royalty income are enabled through license agreements that compensate owners for the use of their intellectual property, creative works, or mineral rights for natural resources like oil and gas extracted from their land. Have you authored a book? Have you written a song? Do you capture really beautiful moments with your camera? All of these can earn you some royalty income.

It can come in as people use them or over a period of time.

A limited partnership is another way to make some cool money without actively working. Limited partnership is a partnership made of two or more partners. The General Partner is directly in charge of running the business. What happens is that the general partner has unlimited liability while the limited partners have limited liability equal to the amount of their investment in the business. Do you own any shares of an organisation? You are earning passive income right there.

Beneficiaries of government payments such as people who are on the Livelihood Empowerment Against Poverty (LEAP) in Ghana. In some countries, people in certain conditions are eligible for some financial interventions from the government. Such interventions count as passive income because they didn't have to actively work for it. Social Security, Child Support, Alimony, Worker's Compensation and inheritance are all forms of passive income.

The last type of income is the portfolio income. It is also known as investment income which simply means we earn such income from investments we have made. It includes interest, dividends, and capital gains on investment. With this type of income, all you need to do is invest in a particular financial instrument and watch as you make money every month, quarterly or annually. Examples include the interest you make on your savings, the money you make when you invest in a mutual fund, index fund, stocks and bonds. Capital gain is when you sell a stock or cash out a pension fund at a higher price or value than you bought or acquired it.

If we are to make extra income, we must acquaint the types of income that are available for us. This way, we are able to determine what choices to make when it comes to finding extra sources of income. Knowing the different types of income helps you know your true financial standing. It also helps you know which type of income is best for you.

Chapter Five

CHOOSING YOUR PART-TIME BUSINESS

FACTORS TO CONSIDER

Before you make a pick when it comes to choosing a part-time business or a side hustle, there are certain factors you need to consider. Passion is a strong reason to venture into any business but that cannot sustain a business. It must not be the only reason why you invest your time and money into a venture headed for the rocks.

We have already established that making money is not the only reason why people look for a side hustle. It is a great booster yet it can also be a catalyst in pursuing something you cannot sustain. Remember, a side hustle is an additional means of making money or an outlet to pursue our passions. We will be looking at some factors we need to consider before settling on that side hustle.

- *Identify your why*
  As we established earlier, there are multiple reasons why people have a part-time business. What is

yours? Why do you want to have a side hustle? This will guide you to make a pick out of the numerous opportunities available for a side business. Do you want a side job to boost your income? It could also be that you need to learn a new skill and find that side hustle as the perfect ground to earn money while learning. For others, a side hustle is the perfect avenue to release their creative side. Another side of them that they want to explore and free. For others, that side hustle is breeding ground for their full-time business.

Your WHY will be the motivator when difficult times come in your business. It should motivate you to drive on towards the goal.

You need to identify where you fall within these reasons to enable you choose your part-time business.

> **Your WHY will be the motivator when difficult times come in your business. It should motivate you to drive on towards the goal.**

- ***Do you have the skill set needed to run your part-time business?***
Before you run frantically with that business idea,

ask yourself if you have the needed skillset to run that business. You cannot seek to apply as a driver on any of the ride hailing apps such as Uber, Yango, Bolt etc without knowing how to drive. That's the basic skill needed. Even if you plan on giving out your car to someone else to drive on any of the ride hailing apps, you need a basic knowledge of driving. What skill set do you currently have? Explore jobs around the skill set you have. You cannot begin a part-time business on skills you lack. Doing that only sets you up for frustration, being a target for rip-offs and ultimately failure.

For people with basic skills on businesses they want to pursue, there is the need to acquire advanced skills. There are tons of resources regarding any path you decide to venture into. Sign up for a course, take driving lessons, perfect your swimming etc. You need to be willing to learn new skills that would help you in your side hustle.

- ***Market Demand***
It is great to have a side hustle but what makes it a side hustle is the fact that it rakes in money or people patronise you. A business without customers or clients who drive demand is bound to fail. For your side hustle to succeed, you need to ensure there is a market demand for whatever service or product you are providing. If you make a choice of

a side hustle based purely on passion, what looks nice to you, what you assume people like, you are likely to run at a loss.

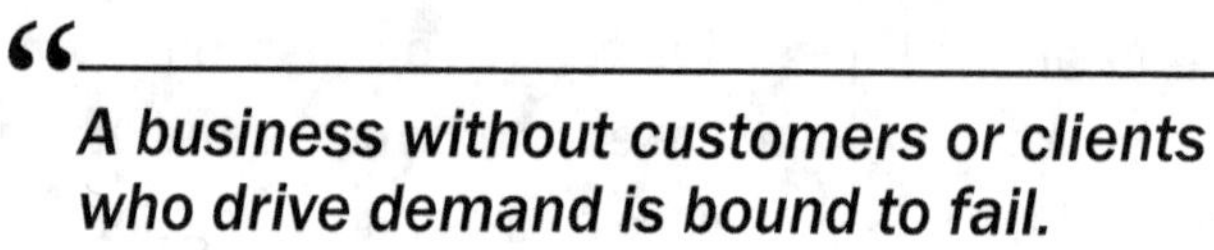

Is your service in high demand? Are you solving the needs of others with your service or product? How close or far are these people who need this service or product you are providing? Do your research; ask potential clients what they want, conduct a simple survey, look at the businesses around you and what they are offering. Is there a gap in the market that you can fill? Can you offer the same product or service others are rendering with a twist or novelty?

- ***Financial implication***

I'm sure you are wondering why this list didn't begin with this point. In my defence, this list is in no order. Also, because I believe sometimes, money is not the first factor when it comes to a side hustle. Most people begin small and scale up, so, it's easier. For many, they save up the necessary capital for their side hustle before they venture into it. However, it is necessary to know the financial implications of venturing into that business before ending in debt or stopping halfway because you did not consider the cost involved.

For any business you want to set up, especially as a part-time hustle, you cannot overlook the financial implication. Some businesses will require much more money than others. Consider the cost of starting up, how long it will take you to make any profit, ongoing expenses and other financial matters. Do a thorough research on the money you will need to start your business. What financial reprieve is available for you in the form of soft loans by non-governmental organisations, government agencies and others. Knowing the financial requirements of your business saves you from plunging neck deep into something you have not planned for. Knowing the financial implications helps you draw a solid business plan with clear drawn plans on your target market and marketing strategies.

- *Legal requirements*
Before you go into any business, do well to check what the law of the country you reside in requires from you as the owner of that business. What licences and permits do you need to obtain before operation? Are there any taxes required from your business? Are there any regulations you need to comply with? What safety and health measures are required of you? What employment laws do you

need to follow?

> **Before you go into any business, do well to check what the law of the country you reside in requires from you as the owner of that business.**

You wouldn't want to fall into the hands of the law while operating your business. This should be strictly adhered to for businesses that cuts across countries and continents. Do your research and adhere to these legal requirements.

- ***Time commitment***

Before choosing a part-time business, consider the time commitment it requires. Some businesses such as cooking for others and planning events require a lot of time. These businesses may require you to work long hours, both during the week and on weekends. Others do not require as much time. Side hustles such as teaching others to swim and babysitting do not require that much time.

It is expedient to consider the amount of time you can commit to a part-time business. Do you have other commitments that require your time? What about your day job? Remember, the rule is that your day job never clashes with your side hustle. If your job is demanding and time consuming, consider something that works for you.

For people with children, do factor that in. If you are a caregiver, factor that in too. You don't want other parts of your life to suffer because of your side hustle. Consider the free time you have when choosing your side hustle.

These are just but a few factors to consider. I believe these factors touch on major salient points everyone seeking a side hustle must look at. These help you make a choice on what side hustle to choose. The next pages will give you an array of side hustles you can do while keeping your day job.

01

START A YOUTUBE CHANNEL

Business Overview

YouTube is the world's largest video hosting platform with a teeming global community of content creators. One does not necessarily need to be an expert in his or her field to garner substantial following. I must hasten to add that being an expert in your field does give you some credence.

Skills needed:

To thrive as a YouTuber, one must be able to write a compelling script, edit videos, and master storytelling. Getting more technical, one needs to know a bit of YouTube SEO, video production which entails lighting, sound design, set design and video quality, graphic designing for creating your thumbnails. One must also know how to market his or her channel, channel analytics etc.

Cost of Starting

Luckily, to create a YouTube costs nada. Nothing. As

long as you have a google account, you are entitled to a YouTube channel. However, that's not all. One would need a high-quality camera which can range from $120 to $500, tripod for $15 to $150, lights (if you do not use natural lighting) ranging between $40 to $200, a microphone for $15 to $100, internet which varies, video creation and editing software which ranges between $0 to $300, registering for courses to enhance your craft which varies. The cost of starting differs from country to country. It also differs from person to person taking into cognizance the fact that different content will need a mixture of different equipment. Someone who creates content on lifestyle may not need as many equipment as one who creates content on fast cars. Interestingly, you can start with your mobile phone if it has high camera resolution or even outsource your production to freelancers which you can get tons of them on Fiverr, Upwork etc. You can run a faceless YouTube channel-I want to give you a little assignment. Kindly go to YOUTUBE and type in faceless YouTube ideas, Trust me, you'll smile and go "wow" when you do so.

How to Make Steady Profit

YouTube is a good source of steady income if you put in the work. Some YouTubers make as much as millions of dollars while others earn a six-figure income. To get the desired income as a YouTuber, you need to churn out consistent content relevant to your audience. The quality of your production attracts viewers who subsequently subscribe to your channel.

To monetize your content, you need to garner a lot of views and subscribers. To help, you can optimize your channel for YouTube SEO (Search Engine Optimization) and promote it. It is best to focus on producing great content and investing in your production quality when you are beginning. That is what will attract viewers to your channel. When your content is good, they will stick and stay, becoming subscribers. Getting these will help you secure a spot in the YouTube Partner Program. This Program allows creators greater access to YouTube resources, monetization features and access to YouTube's Creator Support teams. This means any Youtuber who is on the program earns revenue on ads served on his or her content.

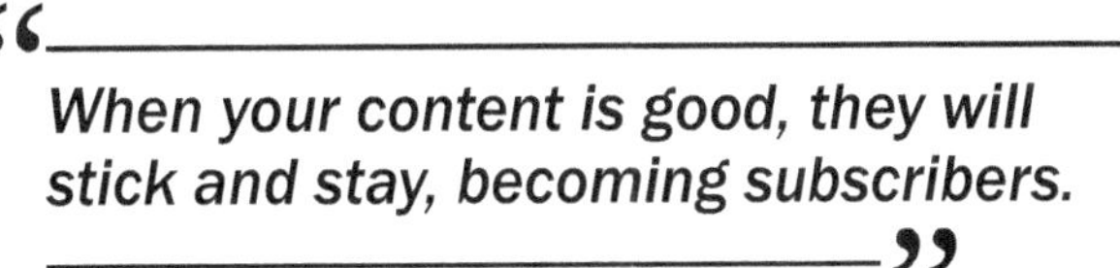

> **When your content is good, they will stick and stay, becoming subscribers.**

Time Commitment

Managing a channel on YouTube can be very demanding. However, it can be juggled with a 9-5 without any of them suffering.

02

BECOME A REAL ESTATE AGENT

Business Overview

Real estate is a venture that has been with us for years. Your job as a real estate agent is pretty simple; help people buy, sell and rent their homes and other properties. With housing needs rising, there is definitely a spot for you in the real estate industry.

Skills Needed

First of all, you do not need a degree. However, you will need at least a high school diploma. A background in marketing will do wonders in this field as you are going to sell. Be a problem solver and an active listener. Learn to manage people as you will be managing both the buyer and the seller. Negotiation skills is a must. Have great communication and organisational skills. Be of good repute.

Cost of starting

In the United States, you may part ways with about $2,000 for your licensing, examinations, fingerprint and background checks. In Ghana, one needs about $250 to join the Ghana Real Estates Professional Standards Association (GREPA). This includes the cost of taking the mandatory exam and the training provided by the Ghana Real Estate Professional Standards (GREPS) Council.

How to Make Steady Profits

Remember this industry deals with a lot of money. The sale of a house or piece of land runs into millions, hence, there is the need to be patient. Generating a lead on someone who wants to buy a property and guiding them to make the actual purchase may take quite a while. However, it is worthy to note that this wait is not in vain as real estate agents can get a commission of 3 to 6% of the purchase. There is also the option of becoming a referral agent. This role requires you to generate leads and hand them over to a real estate agent who continues the process. They earn a referral commission which is a percentage of the agent's commission. Either way, there is money to be made here.

Legal requirements

There is the need to take your country's real estate licensing exam. This differs from country to country. In Ghana, it is vital for an agent to obtain a license from the Ghana Real Estates Professional Standards (GREPS) Council. To get this license, agents must complete and pass the GREPS approved training and examination.

There is also a code of ethics and conducts all agents must adhere to.

Time Commitment

This option is as demanding as you want it. You can take a laid-back posture on the weekdays and go hard on weekends or go hard every day as long as it fetches you the money. Your dedication to the job determines your yield.

> **Your dedication to the job determines your yield.**

03

PHOTOGRAPHY & VIDEOGRAPHY BUSINESS

Business Overview

If you are curious about the world around you and love to capture memories, the photography and videography business may just be the right side hustle for you. With the high spate of weddings, engagements, graduations, naming ceremonies and other events lined up every week, this is a hotspot to make some cool cash.

Skills Needed

You do not need to be a professional to start a career in photography and videography. Attention to details is key. You will need a basic knowledge of photography. If you are great at taking photos of others on your phone or on their phones, you are well on your way. There are many resources on YouTube to help you learn basic photography and videography elements such as lighting, framing, editing etc.

Cost of starting

It may be hard to quote an amount especially because

the price of equipment and software differs from country to country and even from towns to towns. You will definitely need a camera which ranges from $500 to $10,000 depending on the lens and quality. You will need some photo and video editing software too. There are many free ones available for you to begin with and buy more sophisticated ones as you grow. You may need a space for a studio or wait till you grow to get one. An external hard drive is a must have. You will need it to store your videos and photos. There is also the need to build a website to display your portfolio which comprises your work. An alternative is using social media platforms such as Instagram, Facebook, Twitter etc. to showcase your works.

How to Make Steady Profits

Before thinking of profits, you must first be able to decide which kind of photography and videography you want to engage in. There are many options to choose from when it comes to this business; landscape, product, street, travel, stock, wedding, portrait, newborn, event, real estate and pet photography and videography.

The first option to make your profit is to take photos and videos for your clients. There is also the option of selling your photos to others. This works for people who take pictures of streets, travel destinations, landscape etc. You cannot sell photos of people without telling them first. There is the option of selling your photos on platforms such as Shutterstock, Adobe Stock, Etsy, iStock and others. People buy stock photos to use for their blogs, websites, social media posts and others. They are in high demand. An option that allows you keep 100% of your earnings on your photos is having your own website.

Time Commitments

Depending on your niche, it is easy to manage with your 9-5. Stick to appointments as it will help you manage your time better.

04

HOME AND OFFICE INTERIOR DECORATOR

Business Overview

Do you love to decorate the space you find yourself? Are you naturally inclined to create a pleasing atmosphere for people as long as they tell you what they want? you could consider a side hustle as a home and office decorator. Your job is to transform any space of your client into a space that screams their name and meets their needs.

Skills Needed

You do not need a degree or certification for this. However, there are numerous short courses and trainings online that would assist you as you develop. They cover topics such as colours selection, furniture layouts and many more. You will need to be skilful in computer-aided design (CAD) and drawing. This helps you visualise your client's projects. You must have an exceptional sense of design. This means being able to tell your clients what needs to be changed or altered to make their space better and functional. Interpersonal skills, financing and budgeting are necessary skills you need if you will succeed in this field.

Cost of starting

First things first, you need a website. This helps gives a sneak peak of your portfolio to your clients. As a beginner, it is best to start with decorating your own space for a start to begin building your portfolio. The website can cost you from $0 (if it's a gift) to $250. Unless you are drawing your designs by hand, you will need interior designer software which can cost about $560 a year.

> **As a beginner, it is best to start with decorating your own space for a start to begin building your portfolio.**

How to Make Steady Profits

Interior decorators in the United States earn as much as $16.06 an hour. This means, on the average, an interior decorator makes $33,404 in a year. This figure is for someone who works as a full-time interior decorator in the US. With the increased demand for classy, functional workspaces and homes, this field is promising. The income that will be generated is dependent on experience, location, the kind of client you are working for, the kind of project you are working on, qualifications and your marketing expertise. As much as this business does not require a certification, getting a certificate in any related course helps you stand out and wins the trust of clients.

Time Commitments

The great thing about this job is that it offers you very flexible working hours. As long as you have a plan that you stick to and your clients understand, you can do this simultaneously with your day job. You are also able to take on as much or as little job as you want.

DRIVING USING RIDE HAILING PLATFORMS

Business Overview

The practice of paying to be transported from one place to another has been with us for many decades. In recent times, the advancement of technology has made it possible for almost everyone with a car to use that to earn some money through the introduction of ride hailing apps. These are basically mobile applications that connect a driver to a passenger at a fixed charge.

Skills needed

You most definitely need to be able to drive. A smartphone with GPS is a necessity. You need to have an in-depth knowledge of traffic laws if you are going to transport people to and fro. Another skill needed is having a working knowledge of automobiles and how they work. You need to know how to change your tire, understand some basic sounds your car makes etc. You also need great problem-solving skills and interpersonal skills.

Cost of starting

You need a car or not if you intend to sign onto Uber. You need your driving documents in check and working. For Uber, drivers are not required to pay anything to join the platform. For Bolt, you will need to pay GHC10.00 at any of their approved driver activation centres in Accra. The cost may vary based on your country. There is also the need to renew or subscribe to an insurance package for your vehicle.

How to Make Steady Profits

Before engaging in this side hustle, go through the options available to you and choose what works for you. We have Bolt, Uber, Taxify, Shaxi, Yango, Little Ride and so many others depending on your country. Each of these platforms offer a percentage of earnings to drivers on the platform. Hence, it is necessary you do your research properly. Your earnings are a reflection of the number of trips you make and where, when and long you drive. For platforms such as Bolt and Uber, you get your money weekly. Uber allows people with a driving license who can drive opportunities to make money driving even if they do not own a car. There is the option of connecting you with vehicle owners.

Legal requirements

This side hustle requires that you have a valid driver's license. You need an insurance package for your car. Uber recommends a comprehensive policy but allows third party packages. You need a roadworthy sticker and a photo that will be used to set up your profile.

Time Commitment

The great thing about driving as a side hustle is the flexibility it comes with. If you are a morning person, you can utilise the morning rush to your advantage. If that doesn't work for you as a night owl, driving in the night also fetches you some cool cash.

06

WRITE E-BOOKS

Business Overview

What knowledge, story or experience do you have to share? Put it in a book. Reach a lot of people and make some money while at it. What if I told you, you do not need to print your books. You can successfully sell electronic books, popularly known as e-books on many platforms to make the impact you want and earn some income.

Skills needed

You need to know what to write and how to write that in a compelling way to keep your reader engaged. Mastery of grammatical, spelling and punctuation is a must. A working knowledge of how platforms for e-books such as Amazon, Selar, Sayda Hub, BookNook and others work is necessary. Knowing how to talk and persuade people will greatly help you. Having a background in marketing is a plus. Lastly, know the nooks and crannies of various social media platforms.

Cost of starting

The cost of writing an e-book varies. For people who write themselves, it reduces the cost as compared to those who use a ghostwriter. Freelance writers charge as much as $250 to $125 for a book. This applies if the book has between 2500 to 5000 words as writers charge between 5 and 20 cents for per word. There is also the cost of editing, book layout, and inviting cover for the book. Aside these costs, there are additional costs when it comes to marketing the book. Social media campaigns and paid ads, cost of a website for the book (which is advised), and distribution costs. Amazon, Smashwords, and Nook take 30% of your royalties when your price falls within its pricing parameters. BookNook takes about 25%. The total package can cost as high as $500 to $1000 or as low as $125 to $250.

How to Make Steady Profits

Your content must be very good so readers can recommend your book to others. There is the option of making an excerpt a free e-book to whet the appetite of your readers so they can make that purchase. Invest heavily in editing and proofreading. Mistakes throw people off. Your cover design is your signboard. It can make good or bad magic. Market your book aggressively. Use every resource available to you. The ROI is long lasting. Years down the line, you can still rake in some decent amount of money from that one book.

Time Commitments

There is no fast rule to writing a book. You do it within your time as your schedule allows you.

Legal Requirements

You will need an ISBN for your book. You cannot sell your book without it, printed or e-book.

07

GRAPHIC DESIGNER

Business Overview

A graphic designer is someone who creates visual to communicate ideas for all kinds of projects from print to electronic media. They are needed for every kind of project from weddings to funerals. Events of every kind need visuals. That's where the graphic designer comes in.

Skills needed

Basic design skill is a must have. Design principles, ideation, branding, UX and UI Design, typography and designing for print are all hard skills you must have. Creativity will help a lot. Problem solving skills come in handy when clients do not really know what they want. Communication skills, time management, being strategic are all necessary skills you need.

Cost of Starting

You need a computer if you don't have one. The price varies per the specifications and brand you want. You also need a stable internet connection and a source of electricity. You cannot do without graphic design software. There are many options to choose from. Start from the essential ones such as Photoshop, Illustrator and InDesign from Adobe. These can cost you about $12 to $50 per user license each month. You may also need to build a website to showcase your portfolio. There are free sites such as Wix which provides you a free portfolio option. The only downside to it is that the free plan has the watermark logo on it.

How to Make Steady Profits

Start with freelance platforms such as Fiverr which find jobs for you. Upwork, another freelance platform, requires you to purchase credits to connect with clients which costs about less than $15 for about 100 credits. Craigslist is another platform that connects you to clients. You may have to do some free work or personal projects to build your portfolio. Then, take your marketing seriously as this is a very competitive field. You can start out with designs for small events, church events as you scale up to take on bigger projects. There is also the option to design and print on things such as t-shirts, tote bags, throw pillows, mugs etc. It is a great way to make some money. Sell printables such as cards, worksheets, planners, stickers and what have you. You can sell them on your website or Etsy. The more artsy you are, the better.

Time Commitments

This job could be as demanding or flexible as you want it. Take on jobs that you can deliver on time. Do not take on too much so that you do not lose clients or lower the quality of your work. It is easy to combine this with your 9 to 5. You can work on designs after working hours, late in the night, on weekends or early in the morning before your day job starts.

08

DIGITAL MARKETING/ SOCIAL MEDIA MANAGEMENT

Business Overview

A digital marketer is someone who employs the use of varying digital channels to generate leads and create brand awareness. A digital marketer employs the use of various tools to promote a business its products using online channels. A social media manager is in charge of posting new content and engaging with a client's followers on their social media profiles. He or she responds to customers' questions and may create content for a client's social media profiles.

Skills needed

Having a working technical knowledge of social media platforms is a must. For digital marketers, you need to know your stuff regarding Search Engine Optimisation (SEO), Content marketing, UX and UI and data analytics. You also need to possess some soft skills such as listening, collaboration, flexibility, innovation, time management etc. Social media managers should be great at copywriting, communication, community engagement skills, design, public speaking skills etc.

Cost of Starting

You don't need a degree to become a digital marketer or social media manager. However, there are free and paid courses that offer you certificates upon completion. You need a laptop, a stable internet connection, some online tools for online marketing and you are good to go. You also need a blog as a digital marketer to practice and use as your portfolio. A social media manager needs a good phone and a laptop if you can afford it, stable internet connection, and software that will help you. Writing skills, content creation is a must.

How to Make Steady Profits

Digital marketing as a side hustle does not pay almost immediately. You will need to build your network and sell yourself. As much as possible, intern with a digital marketing agency to assess yourself and grow. Do well to define your niche. Specialise in that area and market that. Do you prefer to work for organisations or individuals? Which kind of organisations do you opt for? Establish this so you seek out projects that will grow your portfolio in that area. Join a network of digital marketers who will help connect you to available opportunities.

For a social media manager, your social media profile is your portfolio. Work that magic and let it reflect on your own social media profile. Join a community of social media managers and intern for others.

Time Commitments

If you are great at time management, it is very possible to juggle this with your 9 to 5. Invest in organisers that will help you stick to your schedule.

09

CREATE ONLINE COURSES

Business Overview

The surge in learning online especially after the covid-19 pandemic has led to an avenue to make money for people who can impart knowledge on to others. Platforms such as Udemy, Selar, Skillshare and Coursera make it easy for anyone to create and sell a course to anyone across the world.

Skills needed

You need to be able to teach or impart knowledge to others. Speak coherently and really know what you want to teach. As much as this doesn't require any certification, you need to be sure of what you are teaching others. Actively listening and working on feedback is a needed skill to have.

Cost of Starting

The landscape of online course hosting is diverse with varying pricing models. Every site charges differently for hosting your online course. Udemy stands out as it gives one the freedom to create and host online courses without any upfront charges. It is absolutely free to create and host as many courses as one wants on Udemy. Other platforms such as Selar charge $20 per month to host courses. One would need to own a laptop, stable internet, a camera or engage the services of a videographer to take high quality tutorial videos. There is also the cost of promoting your classes on social media platforms at a fee.

How to Make Steady Profits

Be loud about your course. No one will market your course for you. Pay for sponsored ads on social media platforms such as YouTube, Instagram, Facebook, LinkedIn, Twitter etc. Another way to make steady profit is investing in high quality content. Your videos must be top notch. Your content should not be boring. Engage with your audience. It is an added advantage to know your audience, research on what your competitors are doing and up your game.

On Udemy, there are different revenue sharing models between the platform and the instructor. Other platforms also have similar packages. To make money, people must purchase your course. The more, the better for your pockets.

Time Commitments

You can create a course in your free time. There is no pressure. You can create the entire course at your convenience and market it during your free time such that it doesn't clash with your day job.

10

MUSIC INSTRUCTOR/ TUTOR

Business Overview

Do you know music enough to teach it? Do you know your rhythms, melody, pitch, tempos and other complexities of music? If yes, you may consider imparting that knowledge on to others in exchange for money. Aside teaching in a music school, there is the option of teaching using online media.

Skills needed

Know your stuff. Having a degree or higher education in music is a plus. However, without it, you can still teach others what you know. Excellent communication and presentation skills are paramount. Good organizational and sound decision-making skills are of necessity too. An added advantage is knowing how to play an instrument.

Cost of Starting

For those who want to teach in a school setting, there is the need to pursue at least a degree in music. There is also the cost of owning an instrument of choice. For the online instructors, a laptop and stable internet connectivity is of the essence. There are a few apps such as Moises, Duet Partner, The Studio Director etc. that help while teaching others. Some come at a cost.

How to Make Steady Profits

There are many avenues for a music tutor to make money. Prominent among them is teaching in a school to kids who want to learn how to play the instrument or sing. There is also the option of teaching online to adults in music schools. There is also the option of organising private classes to people who want to learn to sing or play an instrument. Another way to make money is to seek out churches who need the services of music tutors. Many churches need the services of a music instructor to help build their local choirs and other singing groups. You can also create a course and sell on e-learning platforms.

Time Commitment

Teaching in a school may be a bit rigid as compared to private tutorship. The latter is more flexible and can be done in one's free time. Teaching music in a church is very flexible as it can be done in the evenings and on weekends.

11

CAR RENTAL BUSINESS

Business Overview

With the high price of vehicles which seem to be on a consistent upward trend lately especially in Ghana, car rental or car sharing is a service that many yearn for. It could be for making rounds as a tourist, wedding, hanging out with friends and family, work trips and do much more.

Skills needed

You need to possess basic knowledge of how a car works. Knowing how to drive is a must. Great communication skills will help you. Being tech savvy will work to your advantage.

Cost of Starting

You need a car in good condition. You can't rent or share what you don't have. You need an insurance package. Whether comprehensive or third party is totally up to you. I recommend comprehensive though. Find out if your insurance covers renting out your car to others.

You need to ensure your car is top shape so a visit to the mechanic is advised.

How to Make Steady Profits

Start off by telling your family and friends that you are into a car sharing or rental business. This will help them refer their circle of contacts to you. A safer and better option is to enlist your car on a car sharing platform. There are the likes of Turo, Avail, GetAround in the US for private individuals who want to make extra income from their cars. In Ghana, the likes of Wopecar help people with cars who want to make money sharing their cars. Car owners can earn as much as GHC3,500 every month. All one has to do is get signed up on wopecar. com, list his or her car and set their own price. One will be notified of bookings through emails, phone and on the dashboard of the website.

It is better to use platforms like these than doing this on a personal level as it is professional. Damages which may occur are taken care of in a professional way and issues of theft and carjacking are less. Taking care of your car is key to getting repeat customers. Clean and make sure it's in top shape all the time

Time Commitment

It takes very little time to register and sign up to car sharing and rental platforms. For those who want to rent on their own, it takes no time. Maybe, it could take a while to design or get someone to design a flier. Whichever way, it is not time consuming. It is a great way to make some passive income.

Legal Requirements

Every paper concerning your car must be up to date. From vehicle registration to insurance to road worthy, have them all.

12

AFFILIATE MARKETING

Business Overview

Ever referred a friend, family member or colleague to a particular vendor because you loved their services? Did they eventually make the purchase because you spoke to them? If your answer is yes, then you are an affiliate marketer without pay. Affiliate marketing is a performance-based marketing where an organisation or business rewards an affiliate for any customer, they referred who made a purchase. Remember that celebrity who asks you to use their link to make a purchase? He or she is an affiliate marketer. You can become one too.

> **Remember that celebrity who asks you to use their link to make a purchase? He or she is an affiliate marketer. You can become one too.**

Skills needed

There is no certification required. All one needs is the

ability to drive traffic to their affiliate links and earn commission on sales made. This goes without saying that one should have a considerable following on social media. Creativity is key. You would have to whip up new ways to put that affiliate link in the faces of people.

Cost of Starting

The cost of beginning a side hustle in affiliate marketing ranges from nothing to $350 dependant on the tools you use. To begin, one needs a computer/phone, stable internet and dedicated time to grow the business.

How to Make Steady Profits

To make steady money from this side hustle, you can choose to promote products as an affiliate or sell products as an affiliate. The first step is to find products you can promote as an affiliate marketer. To do this, join affiliate marketing programmes such as Amazon Associates or Clickbank. After joining, you will be given a unique affiliate link that you can share with others. When anyone clicks on that link and buys the product, you get a commission.

The other way is to sell products as an affiliate which is also known as drop shipping. This simply means finding a product that you can sell at a higher price than you got it for. Then, you find a supplier who ships the product directly to your customer. After doing so, you go ahead to create a sales page for the product and begin promoting it. When a customer makes a purchase, you keep the difference between the selling price and wholesale price.

Time Commitment

It is a great option for a part time job. Even students with demanding schedules can employ this route to make some money. It's a totally hands off business. Just find ways to get people to make that purchase and you are good to go.

13

PODCASTING

Business Overview

A podcast is a collection of digital audio files readily available for download or listening across the internet. It is basically a talk radio that listeners do not have to tune in to listen immediately. They can listen at anytime and anywhere as long as they have stable internet connection. You can find one on any niche or theme. From health, relationships, gamers to any niche you can think of, there is at least a podcast for it.

Skills needed

You need to possess a great voice. A voice that people will want to listen to. Closely tied to that is the need to be a great conversationist. You must know how to write and interview others. Be an active listener and learn to be a great storyteller. Editing and marketing skills will help a lot. Being tech savvy is a great advantage.

Cost of Starting

There is the almost free option and the option that

leaves you feeling a few dollars light. For both options, you need a smartphone or laptop and stable internet connection. With the free option, the microphone on your phone or laptop will do though the quality may not be as great. You could also use apps such as Spreaker or Anchor on your smartphone. For laptop users, you can use Audacity or Garageband for MacOS Catalina users. For those who choose the path that involves parting with some cash, there are software that assist. An example is Alitu, a podcast maker which goes for $28 a month which offers the user a recording, editing, production, hosting, AI transcriptions, website, music library, courses to help you. There are other expenses such as the cost of a microphone which ranges from $50 to $100, a headphone to help you monitor your recordings, hosting, and a cover art which can be done on Canva for free.

How to Make Steady Profits

Content! Content! Content! You may have the best software but if your content is not good, you will not be successful. Invest in equipment for top notch production. Find your target audience and engage with them. This will help you create a community hungry for your content and giving feedback on how to improve the podcast. They are also a good avenue to get ideas for content they want. Now, you can infuse affiliate marketing into your podcast. There is also the option of advertising products and services of others for a fee. Sponsorship is also one way to make money. You could sell a course, t-shirts and other paraphernalia to listeners. Hosting a live show for your listeners and selling tickets is a sure way to connect and make money while at it.

Time Commitment

This totally depends on the kind of podcast you do and how regularly you release it; weekly, biweekly or monthly. You could also batch produce to get more time on your time.

14

UNISEX SALON

Business Overview

As long as we exist, personal grooming needs will always exist. Taking care of our hair is paramount especially in this age and time when there are different types of hair needs to cater to. That is why we visit the salon daily, weekly, or monthly. Running a unisex salon that caters to the needs of both male and female is a great way to make money.

Skills needed

You do not need a certification or even be a hairdresser. You definitely need strong organisation skills. Have a good grasp on finances and how to keep your books. Great communication skills are a must. As the owner, you need to know how to identify team members and build a team from scratch. Conflict management will come in handy. Attention to detail will save you a lot of trouble. Marketing skills and knowing how to please customers is a no brainer. Having basic knowledge in hair treatment is a plus.

> **Attention to detail will save you a lot of trouble.**

Cost of Starting

This is totally dependent on your budget. You can choose to go big or start small and scale up. Whichever way you choose, you need a location. Your choice of location is very important as it determines if you will be getting a lot of walk-ins or not. Then there is the cost of purchasing equipment you will need for the salon to operate. You will need furniture, hair dryers, sinks, mirrors, shelves, hair curlers, straighteners, towels, hair products etc. There is also the cost of hiring staff for the salon. Do not compromise on quality. Make sure whoever you are hiring is very qualified and has a track record. You will need a hair stylist, barber, manicurist, masseur, a cleaner, a manager and others. This is dependent on how big or small the salon is. You may need to resort to social media to advertise the business to generate patronage and create awareness. There is also the option of placing adverts in the traditional media; tv, radio and newspapers.

> **Do not compromise on quality.**

How to Make Steady Profits

Get a great location that is convenient for your target audience. Invest in equipment. You don't want to lose out on money because you don't have the needed equipment to do a particular hairstyle. Do not neglect the aesthetics. Gone were the days when salons were boring, drab places. Now, people want to create content out of everything including visiting the salon. Invest in interior design. Your workers must be good at what they do. At the end of the day, that's why people will keep coming. Customer service should be top notch. This should be engrained in the minds of all your employees. Thrive on social media. The engagements will do you good and eventually turn into money.

Time Commitment

This is something that you can do part-time as long as you have a competent team in place. A trip to the salon after work or on weekends can suffice.

15

CAREER COACHING AND MENTORING

Business Overview

A Career Coach and Mentor is a professional who helps and guides people who are intent on furthering their career. He or she also helps people who want to switch careers but are unsure of how to go about it. Another part of their job is to help people discover skills that they possess which may be beneficial to their potential employers.

Skills needed

Being an active listener is key. You need to be empathetic to understand your clients. Good communication skills and observatory skills are a must. You must be able to build rapport with people. The job requires you to be non-judgemental and ethical. Having a degree in business is an added advantage as it helps you take on skills like communication, management and operations.

Cost of Starting

The numbers could be as low as $62 to $23,259. Yea.

Aside the money you need to register your business and fulfill all the legal requirements, you will need to part ways with some cash for software. Are they necessary? Not entirely. However, as your business progresses, they will come in handy. Also, they help you to do things more efficiently in less time. Software for email marketing, file hosting, project management accounting and invoicing, social media management and the lot require money. If you choose to operate in a physical location, you need to factor in the cost of a space. This means paying for utilities too. If you are going to have employees, that's another cost. There is also the cost of a website and marketing the business.

How to Make Steady Profits

Discover your niche and reach out to your target audience. Do you want to help women, young people, people who want to switch careers, people who feel stuck in their current roles and want clarity on how to get promoted? Find a niche. You cannot do all at once. Now that you know who you are going to cater to, find ways to reach out to them. Do you need a billboard? Do you need to place ads in the newspaper? Do you need to rely on social media? Are they reachable through email marketing?

You must be good at what you do. To pique the interest of people, you can opt for package prices instead of hourly rates. This way, they do not get discouraged thinking they cannot afford you.

> **You must be good at what you do.**

Time Commitment

You can schedule appointments in ways that they do not clash with your day job. It is a great way to make some cash on the side while keeping your 9 to 5.

16

GHOSTWRITING

Business Overview

Writing is a great way to make money if you are a great writer. You can write for others; a song, a book, copies, articles and so much more. As long as you can write beautifully, you are good to go. Ghost writing is the act of writing materials for others at a fee. Depending on the terms discussed, the client would be named the author without any credit to you or you can be named as collaborator.

Skills needed

You must know how to write very well. That's a no brainer. You can't be a ghostwriter without writing. You must be versatile in your writing style and genres. Have a good command over your language. Time management skill is a plus. Being adaptable will serve you well. Creativity and being able to research and dig the facts are needed.

Cost of starting

You need a computer to write, stable internet connection to connect you to your clients and for research. Constant supply of electricity is also needed. You also need an array of books in order to help with the different projects you will take on. There is also the option of signing up for writing courses to improve your writing.

How to Make Steady Profits

First of all, for anyone to trust you with their work, you must have built an admirable portfolio. Doing this will help you discover your niche. What do you love to write? What have you gotten much praise for? That is your niche. Now, build on it. Network with potential clients who will need your services. You will need to market your services through any medium available to you.

There is also the option of using platforms such as Upwork and Fiverr which helps connect you to people looking for the services of a ghostwriter. On Upwork, one can earn about $20 to $45 per hour on the average with the platform charging a 10%service fee. On Fiverr, you can get from $5 to $50 per hour while the platform charges a 20% service fee. This payment is project based.

Another option is to apply to a ghostwriting firm as a part time worker and take on projects that align with your style. Look around for firms that need writers for projects.

Time Commitment

Flexibility is the rule here. However, that ties in with proper time management skills. As much as you can write at any time, you must deliver on your timelines.

17

WEB/APP DESIGN AND DEVELOPMENT

Business Overview

If you know how to code and do the magic of creating or designing mobile applications, you have the opportunity to make some cool cash. If you are good at developing websites, you are in for making extra cash too. An app developer is someone who writes, develops, tests, and maintain apps for a specific mobile operating system or across a variety of mobile operating systems. The web developer uses programming codes to build websites.

Skills needed

You do not need a degree in either field, however, a degree is an advantage. The alternative is self-learning on YouTube and other resources. By all means, you need to know how to code, knowledge about various platforms and browsers, learn to follow and be up to speed on trending standards of the industry. You should be able to understand user interface of the apps and know how to communicate with your clients.

Cost of Starting

You surely need a computer, a stable source of electricity and internet. The cost of obtaining a degree is hinged on which university you choose and which country you find yourself. An associate degree in web development can cost about $7,000 to $20,000. There is also the cost of other short courses and bootcamps to better oneself. These may last about 14 weeks and cost $11,874. There are also a range of free and paid tools that are available for software developers to choose from.

How to Make Steady Profits

You need to be very good at what you do. Be it app or web development. No one wants to pay so much for mediocre work. Know your stuff. Commit yourself to lifelong learning to keep up with the times and trendy programmes. Time management is of the essence. You can be very good yet not make as much money because you do not respect timelines and deadlines. Anyone seeking your services work with a deadline, respect them. Join a community of developers who can recommend you to others or rope you in on projects.

You can join platforms such as Upwork, Fiverr etc. Check out freelance job sites. It is worthy to note that, it takes time to get your first client. That's why it is great to build your portfolio. Work on personal projects or take on slightly lower jobs. It is a great avenue to build your portfolio. As much as possible, let your portfolio reflect your versatility so that you stand out.

Time Commitment

Things can get pretty intense when it comes to web/app development. To deliver on a project, you need to invest time. As much as possible, take on jobs with realistic timelines that you can juggle with your day job. It all depends on you.

18

TAX CONSULTANT

Business Overview

Tax consultants are professionals who help businesses and individuals manoeuvre the complex world of taxation. They are specialists in tax law and financial related issues. They assist clients minimise their tax obligations and increase their savings. They advise their clients on ways to decrease their taxable income and increase their tax refunds.

Skills needed

A degree in accounting, business, finance or any related field makes a solid foundation though one can do without it. You must be worth your salt when it comes to taxation, accounting and math. Being great at communication is key. You need to be a problem solver and pay attention to details. A working knowledge of various software programmes related to accounting is required.

Cost of Starting

The cost of obtaining a degree is totally dependent on the university, type of programme you are reading and the country you reside in. You do need a working laptop with stable internet and electricity. You may need to buy some software to help you with your work. You may need to join a professional body depending on your country and its laws. This comes at a cost because you need to register and pay some money. In Ghana, the Chartered Institute of Taxation-Ghana (CITG) is the professional body for all tax consultants. Application for membership fee is GHC300 now. Subscriptions range from GHC100 to GHC700 depending on the different categories on their website.

How to Make Steady Profits

Talk to friends, family and acquaintances about your services. What exactly do you do? Do you just file tax returns, solve tax issues with the Internal Revenue Services or offer advice on tax avoidance? Be loud about your services and proudly market them. Go for networking events to socialise and tell your target audience about what you do. Actively seek out small businesses who may need your services. By all means, do join a professional organization. It gives you credence and sets you to meet people who need your services.

Use freelancing job sites such as Upwork, Fiverr etc to secure jobs. Get a LinkedIn account where you share tips on taxation to create a community and put yourself out there. Let your content on social media do the talking for you as you aggressively market what you do.

> **Go for networking events to socialise and tell your target audience about what you do.**

Time Commitment

As long as you know what you are doing, your 9 to 5 won't suffer because you are working on the side. Time management skills are a life saver here.

Legal Requirements

Do well to check the legal requirements of your country before practicing as a tax consultant. In Ghana, it is a crime to practice as a tax practitioner when you are not a member of the CITG. One could face a penalty of paying a GHC6,000 fine to a year of jail time.

19

BLOGGING

Business Overview

Did you know you can own a blog? On what? Anything, from sports to lifestyle to short stories to your crazy tales about your neighbour. Basically, anything is worth writing about. A blog, the shortened form of weblog is an online journal run by an individual, a group or an organisation. It mostly takes on the informal tone and a reverse chronological order.

Skills needed

Basic knowledge of how a computer works, especially Microsoft Word is essential. Knowing how to write is an advantage. A working knowledge of SEO will improve your website's ranking on Google. Know your social media platforms very well. Knowing how to research is a plus. Communication and marketing skills are needed. Basic designing skills will help.

Cost of starting

A functional computer will do. Stable internet and

electricity will come at a cost to you. You need a domain name which is your website address and hosting which is basically where your blog lives. You can invest in a premium theme which constitutes the design of your blog and premium plugins to add to your blog. There are other costs such as buying stock photos and taking courses in blogging to better yourself.

How to Make Steady Profits

Your content must be really good. Depending on the topic, you are covering, know your stuff. Invest in a beautiful design for your blog. It draws people in and your content gets them to stay. There are many ways to make money from blogging. Placing adverts for others on your blog always works. You get paid per views. Affiliate links are another way to make money on your blog. Whether in a review or a post, you include links that earn you a commission when a reader clicks on it and makes a purchase. A sponsored post is when a company pays you to write a blog post about their product and pays you a flat fee not dependent on the number of people who read it. You could also sell products on your blog such as courses, printables, e-books etc. You could also offer services on your blog such as social media management, ghostwriting etc.

SEO is your surest way to get a lot of people visiting your blog aside your content. Consistency in posting is another key. Do not leave your audience hanging. As much as possible, try to post thrice a week. Spend time maintaining your blog.

Time Commitment

You decide when to post and what to post. It is very flexible as you can write a lot of posts and schedule them at your convenience. Whatever works for you is fine.

20

CV/RESUME WRITING

Business Overview

Do you have your way with words? Are you able to turn poor Cinderella into a young beautiful lady fit for the prince? This time, you do it with resumés or CVs. Resumé/CV writing is the art of creating resumés with accurate and relevant information which is professionally formatted and highlights relevant skills pertaining to a specific job. This job is great for writers, human relations people, recruiters and people in related fields.

Skills needed

Writing of course. You should write well. Ability to communicate and understand the needs of customers is key. Basic computer knowledge is key. Attention to details is a plus. Most CVs are written for job applications hence you must understand the job requirement and tailor it to suit the criteria. You should be able to take and receive feedback. There is no need for a degree in the field. I must quickly add, that having a certification is a plus.

> **Ability to communicate and understand the needs of customers is key.**

Cost of Starting

You need your computer, internet and electricity basically to start. You may need to buy templates from sites such as Canva, Zety, Resumé Genius and many others. Grammarly also comes in handy for proofreading and plagiarism. Marketing costs on social media and traditional media must be factored in too. You can also factor in the cost of a website if you can afford it.

How to Make Steady Profits

Referrals work magic. Do some free work for family, friends and acquaintances to get them talking to others about your business. Build your portfolio. Write resumés for fake clients to get started. Refine your own resume to begin with. Networking will help you get new clients. You can also sign up on freelancing sites such as Fiverr and Upwork.

Time Commitment

This job is as flexible as it gets. You can work within your free time. Just manage your time and you'll be fine.

COPYWRITING

Business Overview

Copywriting happens when one writes persuasive content that causes the reader to take an action. It could be to make a purchase, click on a link or donate to a cause. Copywriters are in high demand as they are needed everywhere. From writing for social media posts to copies for websites, emails and advertisements, a copywriter is needed.

Skills needed

You need to learn how to write persuasively. Your writing should be able to get people to take action. This is different from content writing, take note. Aside good writing skills, you need to be creative, have a penchant for research, great communication skills, be attentive to details and be able to adapt. Understanding SEO is crucial.

Cost of Starting

A working computer and phone are needed. You'll

need to read books on Copywriting. Short courses on copywriting are an investment. There are a lot of free courses/videos on YouTube that you can also fall on.

How to Make Steady Profits

Read and practice as much as possible. Create sample pieces for yourself, family and friends. Write sample pieces for sites such as Upwork and Fiverr. As you improve, advertise your services on freelance sites like Guru and PeoplePerHour. Setting up an online portfolio website where potential clients can view your work is a plus. Reach out to people within your circle who need the services of a copywriter. Go for events that have the tendency of widening your circle and contacts. A mailing list is a great tool to employ.

Time Commitment

You can do this within your free time. Your demand determines your work load.

LANGUAGE TUTOR/ TRANSLATOR

Business Overview

Do you have a good command over your native or any international language? Can you speak it very well? Are you fluent enough to teach it? A language tutor is someone who teaches a specific language with emphasis on spelling, language and grammar. A translator translates verbal or written text from one language to another.

Skills needed

A Bachelor's degree in the language you want to teach is a good foundation. Fluency in the language is essential. It goes without saying that you need to possess strong communication skills. Organisational skills are a must. As a translator, you need to be fluent in two or more languages. Excellent writing skills are a must. Attention to details is needed. You must be accurate in your translation.

Knowing the culture of the language is a plus.

Cost of Starting

The cost of obtaining a degree is dependent on your country and the university you choose to attend. You definitely need a laptop, internet connectivity and electricity. You will also need to have some certifications which you need to pay for. In Ghana, you will need a TESOL (Teaching English to Speakers of Other Languages) certificate or a CELTA (Certificate in English Language Teaching to Adults) certificate. There is also the Teaching English as a Foreign Language (TEFL) certificate which equips you to teach English to others online without a degree.

How to Make Steady Profits

Create a profile on all social media platforms and aggressively market your business. There are tons of freelancing sites that you can sign up on. Telling friends and family is always a good idea as it helps you connect with people outside your circle. Get the TEFL certification. It opens you up to opportunities beyond the shores of your country. With that certificate, you can teach English online to students across the world. Platforms such as Cambly, PalFish, Lingoda and a host of others are available for people without a degree.

Time Commitment

Your time organisation skills come to play here. As a private tutor, you can always opt for schedules that work for you. However, as a translator, you need to stick to deadlines. As much as you work within your free time, you should be able to deliver within the agreed timelines. The same goes for the tutor who needs to develop a lesson plan and mark scripts of students.

MAKEUP ARTIST

Business Overview

A make-up artist is someone who uses make-up to change the appearance of someone usually to beautify them. These people are experts in using make-up compounds to conceal, tint and prosthetics to alter the physical appearance of others. Make-up artists are needed to glam up celebrants of weddings, festivals, naming ceremonies and other merry gatherings. MUAs as they are called are also needed on the sets of movies, in newsrooms and even for day-to-day events.

Skills needed

Depending on where you find yourself, you may need a license to operate as a MUA. In Ghana and many other countries, you do not need a license. Knowing beauty trends is a must. You should be able to make your client beautiful when you are done with your brushes. As you will be communicating with clients to get what they want, you need to possess great communication skills. You must be flexible and adapt to the ever-changing needs of your clients. Creativity is a must. Being a team player is a plus as you will most likely be working with the hair stylist or wardrobe stylist.

> **You must be flexible and adapt to the ever-changing needs of your clients.**

Cost of Starting

A phone and internet connection are needed. You cannot do without these. Your beauty supplies are essentials you cannot do without. The brushes, foundation, primer, contour, lashes, lip balm or gloss, wipes etc are things you need in this line of work. Aside people who learn fully on the internet, you will need to pay for training/s to get better. For people who want to get a place of their own for walk-ins, there is the cost of location. You'll need a ring light.

How to Make Steady Profit

Select a niche. What kind of makeup artist are you? Finding your niche will help you know what clients to chase. You are your muse. Start with your face and open it up to friends and family. This helps you create your portfolio and helps you practice as you grow. Network and network. Attend makeup seminars to network with other artists and establish yourself. Change the bio on your social media. It is a great way to get others to see your work. Pay for sponsored ads.

Be adaptable, you may need to do home services for your clients instead of them coming all the way to your office. You will be catering to different people who will pay you differently. Create packages that cater for everyone. As the business grows, consider getting others to help you. This way, you will still be able to cater to a lot of people in less time. Consider getting a YouTube channel to build a community and generate some income on the side. You can also consider selling Makeup products and offer makeup training for new entrants (When you've built a good brand and portfolio) alongside.

Time Commitment
You can work on weekends and your free time.

MC-ing (MASTER OF CEREMONY)

Business Overview

Are you a good public speaker? Can you charge up the energy in a room? Are you able to speak in front of large and small crowds? Then, you may have a career in being a master of ceremony. An MC or Emcee guides and oversees an event to make sure things are orderly, lively and eventful.

Skills needed

You don't need a certification or degree. You must be a great public speaker. Being able to hold conversations with a large crowd is needed. People management skills is an advantage and a necessity. You cannot do this without confidence. Humour is always a great addition. Time management skills are essential.

Cost of Starting

Your confidence and public speaking skills which cannot be quantified monetarily is basically all you need. A phone, laptop and internet connection are needed. You may need a website if you can afford it. Sponsored ads on social media platforms are always helpful. There are many short courses online that will help you grow.

How to Make Steady Profits

Hone your craft. Register for short courses to help you grow. Offer to emcee for family, friends, colleagues at their events. It builds up your portfolio and helps you get better. Aside that, you get to interact with many other people who could become your clients in the future. Research for any event you get the opportunity to emcee. Do your best and give them a show that will guarantee you getting another gig.

Attend events, workshops, seminars and conferences to network with people and introduce yourself as an MC. You can also reach out to event organisers to volunteer your services. Having a website that has pictures of what you have done over the years will help you.

Time Commitment

This is one of the most flexible jobs ever. As long as you are free for the event, you can take it up. There might be times when gigs clash with your day job, but it's totally up to you to take on that job.

25

FARMING

Business Overview

Cultivating the land to feed ourselves and make some money has been with us for as long as we can remember. With the current hike in food prices and the burgeoning need for clean food lovers to eat fresh food, farming as a side hustle can be very rewarding. There are different types of farming to consider. You could opt for fish farming/Pig farming/Livestock farming etc if you are not a lover of the soil. For people who love to till the ground, there are a million crops to choose from.

Skills needed

Know basic farming skills. Understand the farming and agricultural industry as a whole. Problem solving skills are needed. Knowing what technologies are available for you is key. Adaptability will help because you will need it. Management skills are needed irrespective of the size of your farm.

Cost of Starting

You need land to begin. The size depends on you. With crop farming, once you have land, as low as GHC100 is enough to start planting. With crop farming, there is the cost of seedlings, fertilizers, the cost of tools, and the cost of labour.

With livestock farming, the cost is much higher with the cost of starting ranging between 800 to 1,500 cedis or its equivalent in your country. Aside the cost of land, buying the livestock, feed for the livestock and medical care for them are all costs to factor.

How to Make Steady Profits

Thankfully, farm produce sells with little to no marketing. However, some conditions must be met to increase profitability. In your choice of land, choose one that will support your crop. When your land is close to the market, it can rake in a lot of money when your produce is ready. Your land being close to the road or source of transport is an added advantage. Before venturing into any kind of farming, research on the demand for what you want to produce. Is there a demand on the market? How long till you start making money? Connect with stakeholders in the agricultural value chain such as market queens, farm gate people etc. Crops to consider are rice, cassava, plantain, pineapple, beans, ginger, chili pepper and maize.

For your livestock farm, the closer it is to a slaughter house, a market centre, in a city or close to the roadside for easy transportation. Engage with local and international stakeholders who will introduce and open you up to new terrains. You can start with catfish, snail, pig, tilapia, poultry farming.

Time Commitment

This depends on the crop you are cultivating if you are into crop farming. Some crops need much more time and care than others. For livestock farming, you may need much more time especially when they are young. At best, you will need some help.

26

CATERING/FOOD BUSINESS

Business Overview

As long as we live, food is always going to be a need. From breakfast to lunch and supper, there are many options to choose from if you love to cook and can whip up tasty meals. It could something as simple as selling savouries to opening an eatery to catering to people who need meals on a large scale for their homes and events.

Skills needed

You need to know how to cook. Problem solving skills are a must as you will need them. You need to be able to work under pressure because trust me, there will be pressure (Remember a hungry man is an angry man- Just on a lighter note… Haha!). Customer service skills are very necessary in this field. You need to be a team player.

"

You need to be able to work under pressure because trust me, there will be pressure.

"

Cost of Starting

This is dependent on the type of business. Is it a catering business? Is it a restaurant or an eatery? Is it an online business or you have a physical location? There are other costs that will crop up such as buying equipment to cook, buying ingredients, employing people to help etc. You will also need to register your business and get licence and permits to operate as a food business. You'll need start-up capital to undertake a lot of your projects as clients mostly pay some percentage for your services and pay up after you are done. This is the case for most caterers. For small food businesses, that is not the case as clients pay when they make purchase.

How to Make Steady Profits

The food must be delicious. Many food businesses let the food suffer for other things such as aesthetics. Another way to get more customers is to invest in a unique packaging. This can set you apart from other vendors. For people who want to start an eatery or restaurant, do not underestimate the power of aesthetics. Customers who love pictures will troop in. Check your pricing. It is a great way to create a niche for yourself. You do not want your prices to be too high or too low. Research and experiment with prices that work for you and your clients. Market your business. If possible, run adverts on traditional media or sponsor some events or programmes that will give you the necessary publicity. Set social media profiles on various platforms to garner some following and reach out to the general population. Family, friends, acquaintances and work colleagues are a good place to place.

Time Commitment

A small food business is easy to manage. However, as the business grows, you have to get as much help as possible. When you get the right people, it is easy to run alongside your 9 to 5.

Legal Requirement

In Ghana, you need a food and beverage license before operating. In the UK, you need to register with the local council first.

27

DELIVERY/ DISPATCH BUSINESS

Business Overview

The emergence of e-commerce comes with the need for transport. The goal of a delivery business is to get packages of customers straight to them as efficiently as possible without hitches.

Skills needed

You should know how to run a business. Knowledge of how courier services run is key. The ability to lead and work with a team is a great addition. You need to be up to date with the ever-changing technology that couriers use. Customer service skills are needed.

Cost of Starting

You need a delivery van or motor bike. The van should be spacious enough to carry goods. The motor bike should have a cargo box or cargo carrier. You also need a license to operate as a delivery business. There is the cost of insurance for the vehicle and the motorbike. There is also the cost of employing people to work with. You definitely need a smartphone to work with. It helps you navigate the nook and crannies of the city.

How to Make Steady Profits

Find a niche. Are you going to deliver big or small items? This is largely dependent on the type of vehicle you have. Then get in touch with shops and businesses that need your services. Places such as malls, shops, wholesale and retail shops, restaurants, eateries etc. are good places to start. Customer service skills will take one far. In the ugly culture of delivery service providers never delivering on time, being the game changer can make you stand out. This way, you build a good rapport with your clients and ensure you get referrals. Market your business on social media platforms. Sponsored ads would help. Again, adverts on traditional media platforms will also help. There are a ton of online platforms such as Bolt Food as an independent courier. All you need is a valid photo id, a scooter, bike or car and a smart phone. You earn as much as you want as you are paid according to the deliveries you make. There is the option of owning a vehicle to do the deliveries yourself or running a small company where you employ the services of riders and drivers who do them for you.

Time Commitment

You decide when you want to work. If others do the deliveries, you get the orders to pick up and forward to them. For platforms such as Bolt Food, as an independent courier, you decide when to work or not.

Legal requirement

You need to obtain a license from the Postal and Courier Service Regulatory Commission to operate a delivery service in Ghana. There is also the need to have all documents pertaining to insurance, road worthy and others.

28

E-COMMERCE
(ONLINE SELLING)

Business Overview

E-commerce is the act of selling goods and services through an electronic medium to customers. This could be done on a website, on ecommerce platforms such as Jumia, Melcom, Amazon, Ebay, Tonaton, Jiji, etc.

Skills needed

You'll need to know how ecommerce platforms work, especially wherever you market your goods and services. A working knowledge of social media is essential. You should know how to treat your customers right to get them coming back to make repeat purchases. Great verbal and written communication skills are a plus.

Cost of Starting

You surely need a smartphone and a computer if you can afford one. From here, the kind of goods or service you render determines your cost. There is the option of drop shipping where your only cost would be data and marketing costs. There is the option of selling something you produce yourself such as crochet bags, jewellery, etc. Or offering services that you offer yourself such as ghostwriting, graphic designing, designing clothes, hair styling, makeup etc. There is the cost of buying your goods in stock. To build a brand, you may need to spend some money in creating a logo. There is also the cost of running sponsored ads on social media to drive traffic and build your numbers. There is also the option of building your website or joining an existing ecommerce platform.

How to Make Steady Profits

Start out on existing ecommerce platforms such as Amazon, Jiji, Tonaton etc. On Jumia, it takes only five minutes to get registered onto the platform. There is a new seller training for all newbies. Once that is completed, one is given a seller account to manage their shop. Then selling and buying begins. There are a plethora of marketing and promotions available to help one maximise the platform.

If you have your own website, invest in high quality pictures of your goods and services. Let your portfolio speak for you. Make sure you work out the payment systems such that they are seamless and do not inconvenience your customers. You can use different mobile money options, bank accounts, platforms such as Paypal, ZeePay etc. Work on a good courier service to enhance the buying process for the customer. If possible, develop your own delivery system. if that is not possible, partner with a good courier service provider. Consider shipping options too. Of course, if you are into drop shipping, you can skip this. Market aggressively. Run adverts both on traditional and online media. Make the experience as memorable in a good way for your client as possible so they can refer you to others.

> **Make the experience as memorable in a good way for your client as possible so they can refer you to others.**

Time Commitment

Pretty flexible as the sales determines your workflow to a large extent.

FRUIT JUICE PRODUCTION

Business Overview

Fruit juice production is the extraction of natural liquid from fruits and vegetables for human consumption. This can be obtained from the flesh of the fruit or the fruit itself. No extra sugar is added and it is consumed soon after production. With the high rate of clean eating, this business is one that will satisfy the needs of many.

Skills needed

Know your fruits. Creativity is of the essence as you will need to create certain combinations that are unique to you. Customer service skills are a plus. Ability to listen to feedback and work on them will help you greatly.

Cost of Starting

You need a quality juicer. A blender is also essential. Investing in unique but cost-effective packaging will set you apart. You will need a freezer and refrigerator to store your juice. Another cost to consider is a juice dispenser. If you are going to operate in a physical space, there is the cost of location, chairs, tables, shelves, utility cost and so on. There is also the cost of designing a logo, a website if you can afford one and marketing your business.

How to Make Steady Profits

Use the best fruits. Your juice should be good enough to get you repeat purchases. Maintain high clean standards. No one will buy from you when they realise you are not neat enough. If you operate from a physical location, do well to get a strategic location where you attend to customers. It could be close to an office complex, a gym, a school or a church. As much as possible, juice fruits in their season as it can cut down cost in many ways.

Market your business aggressively. Social media is a good place to do that at a low cost. Serving at family and friends events is a good way to start. Partnering with a great delivery system will work wonders for your business.

> **Partnering with a great delivery system will work wonders for your business.**

Time Commitment

You can do this on the weekends. For people with physical locations, you can employ someone to run the place when you are at work.

30

TRAVEL AND TOUR BUSINESS

Business Overview

People require the services of a travel agency who can help them go through the strenuous process of acquiring the required documents they need. If you know your way when it comes to acquiring travelling documents, a travel and tour business may just be the side hustle for you.

Skills needed

A degree in tourism will help. Can you sell products and services. Customer service skills coupled with listening skills are an advantage. You must be one who pays attention to details and be very thorough in all you do. You need excellent verbal communication skills. Administration skills are a necessity.

Cost of Starting

Which type of travel and tour operations do you want to get into. Is it domestic where you sell packages to clients to tour your native country? Will you focus on inbound tour where you sell packages to clients outside your country and bring them in? Are you going to sell packages that allow your clients to travel outside your country for pleasure or business? Then, we have receptive tour which deals only with other travel and tour operators and selling packages to them. Depending on what category you find yourself, you need to at least complete a ticketing course or IATA (International Air Transport Association)/UFTAA (Universal Federation of Travel Agents Association) diploma. There is the cost of renting an office in a good location, registering your business, buying office supplies and equipment. Marketing costs should be considered too. Employing others to manage the business for you is another cost.

How to Make Steady Profits

Partner with bigger travel and tour agencies to cut down on cost. You could help them sell their packages and get a cut. Where your office is located matters. Get a place close to embassies, airports, close to or in tertiary institutions, in commercial areas and in business centres. Invest in customer satisfaction. That leads to referrals and repeat purchases. Research on packages other travel and tour agencies are offering and tailor yours in a better way. Appealing packages do a lot to get people interested. Good and quality service should be your hallmark. No one wants to pay so much for trashy service. Join a trade union; it helps.

> **Good and quality service should be your hallmark. No one wants to pay so much for trashy service.**

Time Commitment

With the right connections and team, you can do this successfully on the side.

Legal Requirements

Aside registering your business, you need a license from the Ghana Tourism Authority in Ghana.

LAUNDRY SERVICES

Business Overview

Clothing is one of the basic needs of man. Closely associated to this need is the need to wear clean clothes at all times. As much as this is a need, many cannot commit themselves to washing their clothes to achieve this. Others detest the very art of washing and would rather outsource it. Laundry service is a system that oversees the washing, drying, folding and ironing of clothes, towels, uniforms, sheets and other forms of garments.

Skills needed

You don't need any certification. However, knowing how to use a washing machine is very relevant. Knowing your fabrics and how to care for them is an added advantage. You should also know about the different chemicals needed for stain removal. Customer skills are a must. Listening to feedback and working on them is an advantage.

Cost of Starting

This depends on the type of laundry business you run. Is it an in-house or commercial laundry? For in-house where you go to the client's house to do the laundry, you may not need anything at all. For commercial laundry where clients drop off their load at your place and pick up when you are done, you need a physical location. For this option, you'll need a washing machine, washing basins, detergents, fabric softeners, an ironing table, a pressing iron, garment bags, clothing lines, pegs, hangers. You also need constant supply of electricity and water. For people who need space, that's another cost to consider. There is also marketing costs to be considered.

How to Make Steady Profits

Start with your family and friends. When they are satisfied, they will refer you to others. Invest in a durable, quality washing machine. You have the option of starting small by washing with your hands. Your service should speak for you. Be as professional as possible. Check your pricing. You don't want to overprice or underprice. Research the prices on the market and adjust accordingly. Do well to satisfy your clients always. Identify your target market and aggressively market to them through fliers, posters, social media ads etc. Stick to your timelines. Do not delay your client unnecessarily. Communicate with your clients if there are going to be any delays. Invest in sweet smelling scents that will leave an impression on your client.

> **Do well to satisfy your clients always. Identify your target market and aggressively market to them through fliers, posters, social media ads etc.**

Time Commitment

This is something you can do after working hours and on the weekends. You also have the option of declining or accepting jobs that come your way.

FASHION DESIGNER

Business Overview
"Fashion is like eating, you shouldn't stick to the same menu." -**Kenzo Takado**

The Japanese fashion designer said the truth. The world of fashion is ever revolving with many needs available to be met. A fashion designer is someone who creates clothes such as dresses, suits, skirts and accessories such as shoes and bags. These clothes should be functional as well as aesthetically pleasing. Clothing has always been a need and will always be. This is where the fashion designer comes in.

Skills needed
Having a degree gives you a strong foundation. Creativity, proactiveness, great sewing skills, being able to adapt to the ever-dynamic trends, great communication skills, being able to work under pressure and accept feedback and work on them are all essential skills to possess.

Cost of Starting

A degree in fashion designing varies dependent on where you choose to study. Without a degree, one needs training in a good fashion school. You will need a sewing machine, preferably an industrial electric machine. There are other things to buy such as threads, scissors, table, ironing board, tape measures, a weaving machine, sketchbooks, pencils, chalks and an embroidery machine. You may need to invest in a generator if you are plagued by erratic power supply. Rent for your shop must be considered unless you are working in the comfort of your home. Costs of advertising and marketing should also be considered.

How to Make Steady Profits

Establish your niche early. Who is your target market? Are you targeting young or old people? Brides or cooperate wear? Every day, casual wear or kaftans? What area of expertise is your strength? Do not end up doing it all. Check your pricing. Keep learning and be up to date with new styles. Being unique and creative will set you apart. If you can afford it, get a website to connect with clients all over the world and display your portfolio while throwing in some testimonials from clients. Spend money on advertisements. A great way to drive sales is to gift some of your designs to a celebrity, an influencer or a model. As they tag your business, it can translate into sales. Invest in high quality pictures of your designs. If you sketched, post both the sketch and the final product. Choosing a great location will help your business. You don't want to be out of town such that it deters clients from coming to you. Build your brand by setting up social media profiles for the business.

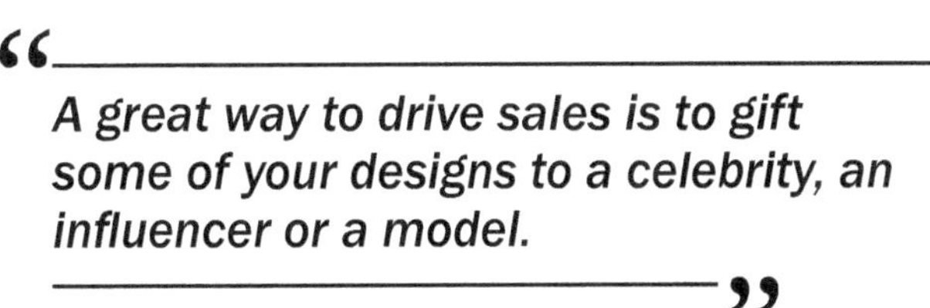

Time Commitment

The time you commit to this business is dependent on the orders you get. You can accept or decline taking on more jobs when you are overwhelmed. There is also the option of employing other designers to help you run the business in your absence.

SHEA BUTTER POMADE BUSINESS

Business Overview

Shea butter is fat extracted from the nut of the shea fruit. It is used in the beauty industry as a salve, moisturiser or lotion. It is also used to aid natural hair growth. Found in many countries in West Africa, shea butter production is something that many indigenous women in areas where the fruit is engaged in. Shea butter pomade is a favourite of many.

Skills needed

Ability to form and lead a team is crucial. You should be able to persuade people to buy your products. Organisational skills are a must. Knowing and understanding how shea butter is produced is essential. Knowing how to add essential oils and other ingredients to shea butter to make it safe is essential.

Cost of Starting

The price of buying the raw shea butter from communities that produce it is the first cost you have to take care of. Now, you have to focus on packaging. Find unique containers for your shea butter. Creating a website for your products ensures that you get a wider reach for them. Invest in aggressive marketing to put your product out there. You'll need to register your product with the Food and Drugs Authority which may attract some charges.

How to Make Steady Profits

Be creative in adding essential oils and unique scents that will set your product apart. You can add coconut oil, baobab oil, hemp and other natural oils to create an array of products. Aside this, find unique and aesthetically pleasing containers for your product. Invest in a user-friendly website with high quality pictures of your product. You can work with models, celebrities and influencers who endorse the product and introduce it to their audience. Use social media to aggressively market your product. Do not set your sights only on the local market. Think global too. Partner with good delivery companies to satisfy clients. Partner with cosmetic shops to stock their shelves with your products.

> **Do not set your sights only on the local market. Think global too.**

Time Commitment

As long as you get in touch with the women who process the shea butter, you are good to go. Packaging can be done in your free time. As the business progresses, you may need to employ the services of others to take care of orders in order to serve customers on time.

Legal requirement

In Ghana, your product has to be vetted and approved by the FDA before you can sell it on the market. In Nigeria, NAFDAC has to do so. Other countries have agencies in charge of that.

Conclusion

These are but a few business ideas that one can run while keeping his or her side job. I'm sure by now, you have fallen in love with one or two business ideas that you can successfully implement without it affecting your day job.

Is it going to be tough? Yes.
Are you going to doubt yourself along the line? Maybe.
Will it be exciting? Undoubtedly.
Will it be rewarding? Most definitely.

You can choose to stick to your 9 to 5 and fantasize about all the ideas you have in becoming the number one hair salon in your vicinity or just go ahead and do it. It's going to be hard but it is hard for every one else. In fact, you are more poised to succeed than someone without any kind of work experience. Regardless of your professional experience and what your side business is, I assure you, you have a heads-up than others who lack professional experience.

Your experience with customers as a front desk executive will work wonders in your ghostwriting side business. You already know how to deal with feedback from customers. You are at an advantage because of your professional skills and experience.

At the end of the day, it is really a plus to build something on the side as you climb up the corporate ladder. You have the hands-on experience of building something from scratch, working to make it grow, learning and unlearning as you build your own empire. Aside the financial rewards you glean from it, you are better suited to take on more at work because of what you do with your side hustle.

I wish you well on this journey of impact.
Go on and make exploits.
The world awaits you!

Resources/References

- https://www.linkedin.com/pulse/regulating-tax-practitioners-ghana-role-chartered-institute-timore
- https://careerfoundry.com/en/blog/digital-marketing/become-a-social-media-manager/
- https://ghstudents.com/digital-marketing-in-ghana/
- https://www.afdvmarketing.com/social-media/social-media-manager-vs-digital-marketing-manager-whats-the-difference-and-which-one-do-you-need-for-your-business/ - :~:text=So%2C%20in%20most%20cases%2C%20the,and%20other%20online%20marketing%20channels.
- https://www.indeed.com/career-advice/career-development/how-to-become-digital-marketer
- https://www.wpbeginner.com/beginners-guide/proven-and-easy-to-start-online-business-ideas-that-make-money/
- https://www.forbes.com/sites/robertadams/2016/10/11/21-legit-ways-to-make-money-online/?sh=79694a3f62d8
- https://vidiq.com/blog/post/skills-become-successful-youtuber/
- https://www.goodfinancialcents.com/home-based-business-ideas-easy-to-start/
- https://www.makingsenseofcents.com/extra-income
- https://www.forbes.com/sites/robertadams/2016/10/11/21-legit-ways-to-make-money-online/?sh=7f2e476662d8

- https://support.google.com/youtube/answer/72851?hl=en
- https://www.linkedin.com/pulse/online-courses-side-hustle-opportunities-advantages-janice-hills -:~:text=In%20conclusion%2C%20online%20courses%20can,knowledge%20and%20skills%20with%20others.
- https://support.udemy.com/hc/en-us/articles/229605008-Instructor-Revenue-Share - :~:text=There%20is%20no%20fee%20to,paid%20courses%20as%20you%20like.&text=While%20we%20encourage%20you%20to,for%20transactional%20sales%20is%20below.
- https://www.entrepreneur.com/slideshow/299326
- https://www.cityam.com/earn-passive-income-22-ways-create-multiple-streams-income/
- https://newsroom.cnb.com/en/personal-finance/financial-planning/create-multiple-income-streams-in-career.html
- https://www.forbes.com/sites/jrose/2017/11/02/different-sources-income/#50dbd27c37bb
- https://www.doughroller.net/earn-extra-income/multiple-streams-income-move-closer-financial-freedom/
- https://thecollegeinvestor.com/16404/the-most-common-multiple-income-streams/
- https://financialmentor.com/wealth-building/wealth-program-system/multiple-streams-of-income/13096
- https://sba.thehartford.com/finance/multiple-streams-of-income/
- https://www.inc.com/amanda-abella/want-to-become-a-millionaire-create-multiple-streams-of-income.html
- https://www.goodfinancialcents.com/multiple-streams-of-income/
- https://hbr.org/2020/03/make-your-side-hustle-work
- https://www.thebalancesmb.com/part-time-home-business-ideas-1794538
- https://www.thebalancesmb.com/supplemental-income-

business-ideas-3514805
- https://www.nbcnews.com/better/business/idea-income-8-books-aspiring-entrepreneur-your-life-ncna940731
- https://blog.hubspot.com/sales/how-to-start-a-business
- https://www.shopify.com/blog/online-business-ideas
- https://www.investopedia.com/terms/t/tipincome.asp
- https://www.investopedia.com/terms/i/income.asp
- https://tipalti.com/royalty-payments/
- https://www.investopedia.com/terms/l/limitedpartnership.asp
- https://www.moneyandmimosas.com/savemoney/makemoneyasaphotographer
- https://photographers-diary.com/make-money-with-photography-side-hustle/
- https://www.laurau.com/interior-designer-vs-interior-decorator-whats-the-difference/#:~:text=What%20Makes%20an%20Interior%20Decorator,visual%20aesthetic%20of%20a%20space
- https://www.indeed.com/career-advice/finding-a-job/how-to-become-interior-decorator#:~:text=Complete%20your%20education,the%20tenets%20of%20interior%20decoration.
- https://design.alyciawicker.com/blog/the-cost-to-start-your-own-interior-design-business#:~:text=The%20cost%20to%20start%20your%20own%20interior%20design%20business%20can,in
- https://bolt.eu/en/support/articles/360001838993-how-to-register-to-drive-with-bolt-in-ghana/
- https://www.uber.com/gh/en/drive/requirements/?uclick_id=892e5a5a-aa8d-46bd-b073-a2141022e7d1
- https://www.uber.com/gh/en/drive/vehicle-solutions/fleet-owners/?uclick_id=892e5a5a-aa8d-46bd-b073-a2141022e7d1
- https://bolt.eu/en-za/blog/how-to-earn-extra-money-with-a-driving-side-hustle/#:~:text=You%20can%20earn%20

whenever%20you,hours%20they%20want%20to%20work.

- https://www.skillsyouneed.com/rhubarb/create-sell-ebook.html
- https://www.crowdcontent.com/blog/content-marketing/cost-of-creating-an-ebook/
- https://www.editionguard.com/learn/how-much-does-it-cost-to-self-publish-an-ebook/
- https://brainstation.io/career-guides/what-skills-do-graphic-designers-need
- https://vitaldollar.com/graphic-design-side-hustle/
- https://brainstation.io/career-guides/how-to-become-a-graphic-designer
- https://kreafolk.com/blogs/articles/graphic-design-business-cost
- https://kitaboo.com/10-steps-to-create-and-sell-ebooks-online/
- https://financialpost.com/personal-finance/business-essentials/creating-online-courses-can-be-a-very-profitable-side-hustle
- https://elearningindustry.com/steps-to-create-profitable-online-course
- https://wopecar.com/
- https://wopecar.com/share-your-car/
- https://mrpocu.com/everything-you-need-to-know-before-renting-a-car-in-ghana/
- https://www.zenbusiness.com/rent-out-car-as-side-hustle/
- https://vitaldollar.com/car-sharing/
- https://adsterra.com/blog/how-much-does-it-cost-to-start-affiliate-marketing/ - :~:text=The%20primary%20costs%20of%20getting,front%20of%20your%20target%20audience.
- https://fastercapital.com/content/Start-an-Affiliate-Marketing-Side-Hustle-to-Bring-in-Passive-Income.html - :~:text=Its%20a%20great%20way%20to%20make%20

money%20online%20and%20can,upfront%20to%20 become%20an%20affiliate.

- https://www.sidehustle.tips/post/money-podcast-2021
- https://podcastle.ai/blog/how-much-does-podcasting-cost/ - :~:text=Assuming%20you%20go%20with%20some,you%20 need%20better%20quality%20gear.
- https://www.thepodcasthost.com/planning/best-podcast-tools/
- https://www.thepodcasthost.com/planning/cost-of-podcasting/
- https://www.thepodcasthost.com/planning/how-to-podcast-for-free/
- https://www.thepodcasthost.com/planning/podcasting-for-beginners/
- https://ghstudents.com/beauty-salon-business-in-ghana/
- https://porterchester.edu/news-events/5-skills-you-need-run-successful-beauty-salon
- https://coachfoundation.com/blog/coaching-business-while-working-full-time/
- https://reference.jrank.org/employment/Mentoring_and_ Career_Coaching_.html - :~:text=Mentors%20and%20 career%20coaches%20are,are%20beneficial%20to%20 potential%20employers.
- https://www.starterstory.com/ideas/career-advice-business/ startup-costs?successful_subscribe=true
- https://www.awai.com/2021/12/become-a-ghostwriter/
- https://www.joomdev.com/5-essential-skills-every-web-developer-should-have/
- https://www.forbes.com/advisor/education/what-is-web-development/ - :~:text=An%20associate%20degree%20 in%20web,type%20of%20school%20you%20attend.
- https://brainstation.io/career-guides/how-to-become-a-web-developer
- https://www.taxghana.org/

- https://www.taxghana.org/index.php/members/subscription-and-other-fees
- https://www.coursera.org/articles/tax-advisor
- https://www.indeed.com/career-advice/finding-a-job/what-is-tax-consultant
- https://smartasset.com/financial-advisor/what-is-tax-consultant
- https://www.productiveblogging.com/blogging-explained/
- https://www.hostinger.com/tutorials/what-is-a-blog - :~:text=A%20blog%20(short%20for%20%E2%80%9Cweblog,an%20informal%20or%20conversational%20style.
- https://www.indeed.com/career-advice/starting-new-job/how-to-start-a-resume-writing-business
- https://howtostartanllc.com/business-ideas/resume-writing - :~:text=Fortunately%2C%20most%20of%20the%20money,just%20under%20%2460%2C000%20a%20year.
- https://work180.com/en-us/blog/10-online-tools-that-will-help-you-create-the-perfect-resume
- https://www.upwork.com/resources/what-is-a-translator
- https://www.internationalteflacademy.com/blog/5-companies-that-let-you-teach-english-online-without-a-degree - :~:text=Yes%2C%20you%20can%20teach%20English,a%20job%20teaching%20English%20online.
- https://teast.co/teach-english-ghana
- https://www.indeed.com/career-advice/finding-a-job/how-to-become-language-instructor
- https://knustnoticeboard.info/how-to-start-a-makeup-business-in-ghana/#:~:text=Makeup%20business%20is%20one%20of,with%20not%20necessarily%20the%20number).
- https://raphaeloliver.com/en/career/discover-the-best-ways-to-make-money-as-a-makeup-artist-and-get-unlimited-profits-on-the-internet/

- https://www.skillsacademy.co.za/how-to-start-a-business-as-a-freelance-makeup-artist/
- https://www.linkedin.com/advice/0/how-do-you-find-emcee-opportunities-skills-emcee - :~:text=One%20of%20the%20best%20ways,organizers%2C%20speakers%2C%20or%20performers.
- https://socastin.com/10-essential-qualities-of-a-professional-compere/ - :~:text=He%20must%20have%20an%20easy,does%20the%20same%20to%20another.
- https://www.pulse.com.gh/news/meet-kabutey-my-mc-why-emceeing-is-now-a-big-business/nzcr4h2
- https://africabusinessideas.com/how-to-start-farming-business-in-ghana/ - :~:text=Farm%20business%20in%20Ghana%20is,has%20to%20eat%20to%20survive.
- https://thefarmdreams.com/10-profitable-farming-ideas-in-ghana-2022/
- https://www.indeed.com/career-advice/career-development/farmer-skills
- https://in.indeed.com/career-advice/career-development/farmer-skills - :~:text=Skills%20like%20problem%2Dsolving%2C%20interpersonal,cultivating%20crops%20and%20fixing%20machinery.
- https://africabusinessideas.com/how-to-start-restaurant-business-in-ghana/ - :~:text=The%20actual%20cost%20of%20running,25%2C000%20%E2%80%93%2040%2C000)%20Ghana%20cedis.
- https://bolt.eu/en-gh/food/courier/
- https://ghanainsider.com/how-to-start-a-delivery-service-in-ghana/
- https://africabusinessideas.com/start-a-delivery-business-in-ghana/ - :~:text=%E2%A6%81%20Make%20ready%20a%20delivery,need%20of%20your%20delivery%20service.
- https://pcsrc.gov.gh/licensing-requirements/

- https://group.jumia.com/business/marketplace/sell
- https://www.usabusiness.co.in/best-e-commerce-websites-in-ghana/
- https://synder.com/blog/how-to-start-an-e-commerce-side-hustle/ - :~:text=When%20you%20understand%20the%20importance,This%20guide%20is%20for%20you.
- https://www.profitableventure.com/equipment-start-juice-bar/
- https://www.businesscoachphil.com/how-to-start-a-travel-and-tour-agency
- https://www.ghanabusinessweb.com/blog_detail/19/how-to-start-a-travel-agency-business-in
- https://africabusinessideas.com/how-to-start-travel-and-tour-business-in-ghana/
- https://nationalcareers.service.gov.uk/job-profiles/travel-agent
- https://africabusinessideas.com/how-to-start-laundry-business-in-ghana/
- https://www.owogram.com/laundry-service-business/
- https://femmefrugality.com/laundry-care-side-hustle/
- https://www.harpersbazaar.com/fashion/designers/a1576/50-famous-fashion-quotes/
- https://www.indeed.com/career-advice/finding-a-job/how-to-become-fashion-designer-without-a-degree
- https://riohs.com/a-beginners-and-professionals-guide-to-become-a-fashion-designer-in-ghana-13-steps-to-success/
- https://www.informationhood.com/how-to-start-a-fashion-design-business-in-nigeria-and-ghana/
- https://fortmi.com/how-to-start-a-fashion-designing-business-in-ghana
- https://www.mondaq.com/life-sciences-biotechnology--nanotechnology/1093028/how-to-register-cosmetics-in-ghana-